Praise for
Embracing Life After Loss by Allen Klein

"Serendipitously, I was asked to review Allen Klein's book *Embracing Life After Loss* directly following my mother's passing. Reading this book has been a gift to me during this difficult transition. As the sting of loss begins to wane, the words in this wonderful book continue to resonate in my heart and in my healing. This book does the impossible—it turns the dark into something beautiful. This is a moving, provocative book about life, death, and most importantly, perspective."

—Joseph J. Luciani, author of *Self-Coaching: The Powerful Program to Beat Anxiety & Depression*

"If life sometimes feels like a bucket full of small dark stones, Allen Klein's insights are like bright pennies waiting to be found. This collection of brief sermons on grief and recovery can help turn fear into forgiveness, wounds into wisdom, and losses into laughter."

—Stephen Kiernan, author of *Last Rights*

"This book is a wonderful companion in your darkest hours. It feels like a warm, nourishing hug from a dear and loving friend. It will soothe your heart and warm your soul. It will help you to find that sacred place within you that is never lost and never changes—your spiritual heart be gracefully awakened through the mystical, transformational, holy experience of laughter."

—John E. Welshons, author of *When Prayers Aren't Answered*

"Like a dear friend, this beautiful book takes us by the hand and walks us through the stages of loss and recovery. Allen Klein has inspired us all to define ourselves, not by our grief, but by our joy."

—Susan Sparks, Pastor, author of *Laugh Your Way to Grace*

"This is an easy-to-read, compassionate, and useful book for dealing with loss and grief. Allen Klein addresses different aspects of the grieving process, all of which speak to the heart of what it is to deal with and recover from loss. This is a wonderful addition to the current literature on grief and would make a wonderful condolence gift."

—Judy Tatelbaum, author of *The Courage to Grieve*

"Raising Lazarus from the dead is less miraculous than raising ourselves from the loss of a loved one. Allen Klein, invoking his decades of experience 'lightening the load of grief' offers an unexpected grace, a slight levitation of the heart, into the healing process."

—Stephen Levine, author of *A Year to Live*

"With great love and humor, Allen Klein shares his wisdom, wisdom which shows us the path to healing the wounds uncovered by our grief, wisdom that he has clearly earned through his own deep practice. He walks the walk. We are all grieving. Allen shows us the way, as Rumi says, to use grief as the garden of compassion."

—Dale Borglum, Executive Director of the Living/ Dying Project

"Klein has written a poignant and easily readable guide to the grieving process based on his personal and professional experiences. Grieving people will find some solace and professionals will gain insight from someone who has been on both sides of grieving and helping the bereaved."

—Stephen R. Connor, author of *Hospice and Palliative Care: The Essential Guide*

"As a hospital chaplain I witnessed the unwelcome burden that grief added to a person's life. In his book, Allen Klein gives a realistic and sensitive vision that will sustain the hope necessary for grief's journey."

—E. T. (CY) Eberhart, author of *In the Presence of Humor*

"Whew…what a book! Allen sings a simple song: embrace life, remember the joy, and find gratitude in knowing you have been loved."

—Steve Rizzo, author of *Becoming A Humor Being*

"Allen Klein has such a beautiful perspective! His book is an important, authentic, and liberating look at how we can move through loss with compassion, humor, and peace. If you're dealing with a loss of any kind, this book will support you in your journey."

—Mike Robbins, author of *Be Yourself,*
Everyone Else is Already Taken

"Allen Klein is a counselor, a philosopher, a theologian. His pain, from losing his young wife, and his healing, from moving beyond her death, are evident in every word he writes. In easy-to-take doses, he offers practical advice on seeing the light in the darkest of times. He shares the secret that survivors—of everything from cancer to the Holocaust—have learned."

—Steve Lipman, author of *Laughter in Hell*

"There are very few books that everyone can identify with and benefit from. This is one of those books. We've all experienced a loss that leaves us dispirited and adrift. *Embracing Life After Loss* recognizes that even on hallowed ground, we lose our footing and our bearings. Allen Klein encourages us to find our way and teaches us the five 'stages of living' after loss, so that we can not only survive, but thrive, enjoy, and embrace our lives."

—Alan Gettis, author of *It's All Part of the Dance:*
Finding Happiness in an Upside Down World

"Klein's lucid writings make compelling connections with
psychology, religion, history, philosophy, and good ol'
common sense. His personal experiences, clinical examples,
and delightful humor is like viewing a trapeze artist who lets
go of one rope, and gracefully takes hold of another, without
a misstep. This is a penetrating treasure trove of profound
insights and skillfully blended constructed tools."

—Earl A. Grollman, author of
Living When a Loved One Has Died

Embracing Life After Loss

Also by Allen Klein:

You Can't Ruin My Day
The Art of Living Joyfully
Change Your Life!
Having the Time of Your Life
Always Look on the Bright Side
Words of Love
Inspiration for a Lifetime
The Healing Power of Humor
The Courage to Laugh
Secrets Kids Know...That Adults Oughta Learn
L.A.U.G.H.: Using Humor and Play to Help Clients Cope

Embracing Life After Loss

A Gentle Guide for Growing Through Grief

Allen Klein

Foreword by Gloria Horsley, PhD,
President and cofounder of Open to Hope

Mango Publishing
CORAL GABLES

Cover Design: Jermaine Lau
Cover Photo: HelloRF Zcool (Shutterstock)
Layout & Design: Roberto Núñez

Lyrics from the song "You're There," lyrics by Alix Korey, music by David Friedman,
©MIDDER Music Publishing, Inc. Used by Permission. All Rights Reserved.

For permission requests, please contact the publisher at:
Mango Publishing Group
2850 S Douglas Road, 2nd Floor
Coral Gables, FL 33134 USA
info@mango.bz

For special orders, quantity sales, course adoptions and corporate sales, please
email the publisher at sales@mango.bz. For trade and wholesale sales, please
contact Ingram Publisher Services at customer.service@ingramcontent.com or
+1.800.509.4887.

Embracing Life After Loss: A Gentle Guide for Growing through Grief

Library of Congress Cataloging-in-Publication number: 2019931489
ISBN: (print) 978-1-64250-006-6, (ebook) 978-1-64250-007-3
BISAC category code: SEL010000, SELF-HELP / Death, Grief, Bereavement

Printed in the United States of America

To hospices everywhere,
who do incredible work with the dying,
the grieving, and their families.

I always try to balance the light with the heavy; a few tears of human spirit, in with the sequins and the fringes.

—Bette Midler, American entertainer

Table of Contents

Step Two

Learning **50**

Step Three

Step Four

Step Five

Foreword

Through our Open to Hope Foundation, with the mission of helping people find hope after loss, we have interviewed thousands of bereaved people and read hundreds of grief and recovery books. We have found Allen Klein's understanding of the grieving process, and his focus on humor as a healing tool, to be a great addition to the recovery literature.

In this heartwarming book, *Embracing Life After Loss*, Allen gently walks us through the journey of grief, loss, and recovery. He gives us great and much needed advice but also inspires us through quotes and personal experiences. And he doesn't miss a beat as he covers the major issues facing the bereaved, including self-forgiveness.

Allen guides us through five stages of going from loss to laughter…losing, learning, letting go, living, and finally, laughing. I know that laughter was a healing part of my grieving process after the death of our beloved son Scott, at age seventeen. Allen's promptings have inspired me to tell a funny story about my son prior to his death.

My daughter Heidi was off to her freshman year of college. Her brother Scott was a junior in high school. Heidi asked if she could take a small portable television to college with her. As it happened, the television set was residing in Scott's room. We agreed that she could take the television set, but when it was time for her to leave she found the set handcuffed to Scott's bed and Scott nowhere to be found. Needless to say, the television set never left the house.

No doubt Allen's writing will lift your spirit and inspire you to remember and share heartwarming and funny stories of those you have loved and lost. Thank you, Allen, for sharing your life, love, and humor with the world. You're a one-of-a-kind treasure.

Gloria Horsley, MFC, CNS, PhD
President and cofounder of Open to Hope

Dear Reader

While this book comes out of the lessons I've learned about loss from the death of my wife, the thoughts within address all kinds of loss. The feelings that often accompany the loss of a loved one also apply to such things as losing a pet, getting a divorce, being let go from a job, or any other major setback in your life. Any loss can be overwhelming. The aim of this book is to help you realize that loss is part of life, that it can be one of our greatest teachers, and that, in spite of your loss, you can once again fully partake in what life has to offer.

After my wife died at the age of thirty-four, I was devastated. I went for counseling to deal with my grief. After three sessions, the therapist told me that life is difficult. I fired him. I walked out of his office. I didn't need to hear that. I was living it.

I also sought out books about grief. I thought that they would help me understand my loss. Most of them did not. They were huge tomes, more than I could handle at the time. Most of them told me how horrible I might feel after losing a loved one. That I might not have my appetite, not sleep well, and/or be depressed.

That advice did not help me deal with my grief. I needed something that was easy to read. Something that provided encouragement. Something I could turn to on a daily basis for inspiration and uplifting thoughts. Something that spoke to my heart, not my head. Finding none of that in most grief books, I wrote my own. It is the book you are either holding in your hand or reading in a digital format.

My intention for the book is that it will provide comforting, heartfelt thoughts and a lighter tone not found in other books on loss. I also hope that it will show you that there can be a positive side to loss and help you understand that, although your loss is a life-changing experience, it need not necessarily be a negative one. And that, because of life's brevity, a loss can be a powerful wake-up call to celebrate life.

Please note that I am not advocating avoiding the grief caused by loss or rushing through it. Unexpressed grief can come back again with a stronger force. It is important to fully deal with the grieving process after a loss. However, my goal in writing this book is to help you go beyond your loss to embracing life fully again and, yes, even laughing again. And to help you go from merely surviving to thriving. Also, I hope that it will uplift your spirit, touch your heart, and nourish your soul.

P.S.: The advice in this book is what worked for me during my time of loss. Some of it may seem right for you, some of it may not. As with any information, take what fits and leave the rest behind.

Opening Diary

Sunday, June 24

I have no sisters. I do, however, have a cousin who has been like a sister to me. We grew up together, shared many a happy moment at a Broadway show, and enjoyed numerous fun-filled meals together. And even though she lived on the East Coast and I on the West, we were very close.

Three days ago, I found out that she has leukemia. And, at her age of seventy-eight, the doctor doesn't think the prognosis is very good.

I am very upset. I have not only felt like crying in the past few days but have actually done so several times. And while I haven't consciously tried to find some humor in the situation (I am still in shock), there is a picture hanging on my wall in the hallway that brings a small smile to my face every time I see it.

It is of Bernice and some Disney-like character. The oversized bird's bright yellow beak and Bernice's nose are touching. Her face is glowing with laughter and joy.

This photo is the essence of Bernice's spirit—upbeat and playful. It is a wonderful reminder to me that, although Bernice's body may be going through turmoil right now, her bright spirit will remain forever.

Wednesday, July 4

Thoughts of Bernice are all-consuming. I wake up at night thinking of her. Every time the phone rings, my fear is that there is some bad news.

Wednesday, July 11

I'm out of town, attending a week-long conference in San Diego, California. The phone in my hotel room rings at two thirty in the morning. Without even answering it, I know exactly what has happened. I check out of the hotel and I'm on a plane to New York to arrange for the funeral and Bernice's burial.

Friday, July 13

Bernice's coffin is lowered into the ground. It is Friday the 13th.

Saturday, July 14

The day after the funeral, my daughter and I decide we need some quiet time together. We stay around Bernice's apartment going through some of her possessions. In the afternoon, we take advantage of the unusually cool, for New York, summer weather and go to a nearby museum. There we spend time reflecting in a tranquil setting.

But the tranquility doesn't last long. Unbeknownst to us, it is the museum's annual fundraiser. When we enter the museum's courtyard, hundreds of people are starting to gather. The DJ is working his musical magic, the band is getting ready to take over, and the crowd is anticipating the loud and lively late afternoon.

We get caught up in the festive scene, order a beer, and delight in watching the spectacle of the young New York art scene. There we sit, forgetting—at least for a while—that Bernice's funeral occurred just a little over twenty-four hours before.

We also realize that the solitude we planned for that day was not to be. When the loud music gets a bit much for us, and the crowd starts to become overbearing, we head for one of Bernice's favorite neighborhood restaurants. Just before our meal arrives, a young man takes a seat next to our table. With his guitar, he plays and sings songs by the Beatles, Paul Simon, and others. He invites us to sing with him. We do. Like the museum experience, the quiet dinner we anticipated did not happen.

But what did happen was spontaneous magic. Throughout the day, it was as if Bernice's luminous spirit was saying to us,

"You've cried enough. You've mourned enough. Now it's time to partake in the music of life."

Sunday, July 15

I think of two things Bernice told me. One she shared several months prior to her death. She said that she lived her life by what her mother taught her—to bring joy to at least one person each day.

The other thing she told me occurred when I was a teenager. It was about her world excursions. She was the first person I knew who traveled by airplane. I used to stand on the observation deck at LaGuardia Airport and wave to her as her plane took off. One day, I asked her if she was afraid that the plane might crash.

She said she wasn't, but that if it did, she would want it to be on the return flight so that she would not miss a moment of her vacation. That was Bernice—never missing a moment of what life had to offer.

Thursday, Friday, Saturday...July, August, September...and the rest of the days.

I think of Bernice often, and with the music of her joyous spirit to guide me, I get on with life.

Step One

Losing

> *If you believe yourself unfortunate, because you have loved and lost, perish the thought. One who has loved truly, can never lose entirely.*
>
> **–Napoleon Hill, American author**

Losing a loved one is not easy. I know—I have had many losses in my life. The one that made the most impact on my life was my wife's death when she was thirty-four. In addition, my mother, my father, my four grandparents, my sister-in-law, several cousins, and both my mother-in-law and father-in-law have died, as well as over forty friends and colleagues who are no longer here because of AIDS or cancer.

I don't think we ever forget the people we lose. So in some sense, they are never gone. But, still, it hurts not to be able to see them, hear them, or hold them again.

Loss hurts. But it can also help us be stronger, wiser, and, if nothing else, more appreciative of every moment we have on this earth.

In Shock

If you're going through hell, keep going.

–Winston Churchill, British politician

When a loss occurs, shock sets in. This is natural. At the time, it may feel like you can't deal with life. That is okay…for now.

You may feel numb and listless.

You may not want to eat or even get out of bed in the morning.

You may feel overwhelmed.

You may feel that your life has stalled or stopped.

You may also feel angry, depressed, and even guilty.

Know that you are not going crazy. All of these are normal responses in the grief process.

Why Me?

*I don't know why babies are born with AIDS, young
people get killed in tragic accidents, or the Cubs
can't win a World Series. But I do believe there are
blessings in every challenge, and lessons, growth
and ultimately prosperity in what they bring us.*

–Randy Gage, American prosperity teacher

After experiencing a loss, you may be asking yourself, "Why
has this happened to me?"

The answer to the "why me" question is twofold. First, perhaps
there is no answer to that question. And second, you are too
close to your loss right now to know the answer. While these
answers don't provide much comfort, some solace might
be had in knowing that we are all a small part of a much
grander universe and that, with time, your loss will take its
proper place.

Perhaps, too, the better question (or questions) to ask after a
loss might be:

- "How will this help me live more fully knowing that my
time is limited too?"

- "How will this help me contribute to the greater good for all people?"

- "How will this make me become a more loving person?"

Rising Above Your Loss

What is extraordinary about us is that we each have the capacity to rise like the phoenix out of our ashes, to create ourselves newly, to begin again. We can transform ourselves and our lives, regardless of what we have endured before now. Maybe the true purpose of suffering is that out of our pain, we will rise, expand, grow, and achieve.

—Judy Tatelbaum, American author/therapist

Go ahead. Wallow in your loss. It is okay. You probably need that right now. But that is now, not forever. Somewhere down the road, your tears will subside.

When we experience a loss, we can focus on the tears and on what we no longer have, or we can appreciate what we still have. We can focus on a life cut short or celebrate a life lived. We can feel sorry for ourselves or see our loss in a larger context.

You can get lost in your loss; you also have the power to rise above it.

During loss, it seems that you can't possibly go on. Everything in your life may seem like it has come to a standstill. But you can go on—and will go on.

The Big Picture

The next time you are feeling bored, despondent or irritable, try to remember your cosmic situation; at this moment you are riding on a big round-shaped rock that is hurling through space, spinning around its own axis at about a thousand miles per hour and spinning around the sun at approximately 66,000 miles per hour. Along with our entire solar system, you are also soaring through the Milky Way galaxy at nearly 500,000 miles per hour. And what's truly remarkable is that you don't even have to hold on.

–Wes "Scoop" Nisker, Buddhist teacher

I recently went to the planetarium in San Francisco. I saw an incredible astronomical show about the creation of our sun. I learned that the sun is actually a star and that it is the nearest star to earth. I also learned that it was created 4.6 billion years ago. And it will burn itself out in another five billion years.

Fascinating numbers, but I could not wrap my mind around them. They were talking about billions of years ago and billions of years into the future. I couldn't even imagine what one million years would look like, let alone billions.

It made me realize what a small speck we are in the history of our vast universe. And how trivial some of the things we concern ourselves about really are. It also helped put my losses, which seem so overwhelming at the time, in perspective.

You may feel that your loss is the largest thing in the universe. In time, and with perspective, your loss will take its proper place in your life.

Triumphing Over Tragedy

The soul would have no rainbow had the eyes no tears.

–John Vance Cheney, American poet

Life can be filled with joy. It can also be filled with immense sadness. Our ups and downs during life's journey depend on a number of factors. These include such things as our circumstances, our reactions to our circumstances, and yes, even luck. Often we can't control our circumstances, or our luck, but we can control our reactions to what happens to us and, by doing so, overcome them.

There have been numerous books, articles, and movies about people who have risen above the difficulties that life has handed them. They have won gold medals running races with no legs, they have gone from the bottom of the heap to the top of the boardroom, and they have been devastated by the loss of a loved one. Many of them have gone on to inspire others or create organizations—like Mothers Against Drunk Drivers—to fight against the injustice that caused their loss. They have all triumphed over tragedy.

These are no superheroes. These are ordinary people who realized that they might be down, but they didn't have to stay there. They too have had feel-like-crying moments, perhaps many of them. But they didn't let those times dictate their future. They eventually took those setbacks and, at some point, realized that they could surmount them.

If those people can do it, you can too.

Endings Are Also Beginnings

*The world is round and the place which may seem
like the end may also be only the beginning.*

—Ivy Baker Priest, American politician

You can't turn back the clock and undo your loss. But you
can move forward by realizing that, when one door closes,
another opens.

After my wife died, I had no idea where my life would lead
me. I knew that my world had changed, but I didn't know
where it was headed. What I did know was that I had to trust
the process.

The death of my wife led me first to hospice work and then
to the investigation and teaching of the therapeutic value
of humor. It wasn't a journey I signed up for, understood,
or wanted, but, looking back, it showed me that out of
death comes new life. And those setbacks often become
stepping stones.

Your loss is a milestone that has made a major impact on your
life. It has ended a world you once knew. But, at the same
time, it has created new opportunities and an opening for the
beginning of a yet-to-be-discovered world.

Death Is Part of Life

To everything there is a season, and a time to every
purpose under heaven:
A time to be born, and a time to die.

—Ecclesiastes 3:1–8, Old Testament

Everything that lives also dies. If you are reading this book, you are alive. And if you are alive, someday you will die. While we may want it to be otherwise, that is the nature of all beings. Death is not something separate from life; it is a part of it.

You might think that, in a perfect world, no one would die. That may seem like an ideal situation, but it is just the opposite.

Imagine, for a moment, a world where no one dies. It would be chaotic and unlivable. If no one died, there would not be enough places for people to live. There would not be enough food. There would not be enough jobs. There would not be enough natural resources to support humanity. And, would anything ever get accomplished knowing that there was an unending amount of time to get things done? Would people even value life knowing that it went on forever?

So, although death brings grief, it is a necessary evil. In fact, on some level, death is nature's way of keeping the world in balance.

Loss is also necessary to help us grow spiritually. Yes, loss hurts, but it can also help us be stronger, wiser, more compassionate, and if nothing else, more appreciative of every moment we have on this earth. And, while nothing can bring back your loved one, knowing that the loss is part of a vast universal truth may bring some comfort.

The Hero's Journey

*A hero is an ordinary individual who finds
the strength to persevere and endure in
spite of overwhelming obstacles.*

—Christopher Reeve, American actor

Joseph Campbell, the American mythologist, says that part of
the human experience involves suffering certain losses, leaving
our predictable comforts, and setting out into unfamiliar
terrain. Inevitably, we meet with things that block our way and
take us into dark places to do battle with unseen forces. Out of
these struggles, we emerge with wisdom. Campbell is talking
about the "hero's journey."

After a loss, you are on a hero's journey. You are in unfamiliar
territory and in an uncomfortable place. You have come to
a major challenge in your life and a very dark place. You are
battling unfamiliar forces, and as in the hero's journey, you will
emerge with greater wisdom.

It may not seem like it right now, but you too are a hero.

Ask the Horse

*Life is what happens to us while we
are making other plans.*

–Allen Saunders, American writer/cartoonist

There is an old Zen story about a man riding a galloping horse. Seeing him whizzing by, a woman shouts to the man, "Where are you going in such a hurry?" The man yells back, "I have no idea. Ask the horse!"

Most of us go through life making plans for the future despite the fact that none of us really know what the future will bring.

For many years, my wife and I wanted to live in San Francisco. My wife was from there. We would visit her parents at least once, sometimes twice, a year. We would come back home from our trips and I would draw pictures of Victorian houses. Someday, I thought, we would own one of them.

After there was a fire in our New York City apartment building, we decided to move to San Francisco—the city of our dreams. A few years after that, we bought a Victorian house that was built in 1876. Then we found out that my wife had a rare life-challenging liver disease. There were no liver transplants at the time and there was nothing that could be done for her. She died three years after the diagnosis.

That wasn't in our plans. We were supposed to live happily ever after in the house we always wanted in the City by the Bay. But it was not to be. I was riding the horse in the direction I wanted to go, but the horse was going in a different direction.

Right now, you may feel that what has happened to you is the worst thing in the world. But that is because you can only see the present moment. Be patient. Down the road, you will see where the horse is headed.

One Step at a Time

One step at a time is good walking.

–Chinese proverb

I have always been dubious when I read that some entertainer is supposedly an overnight sensation. How absurd; there are no overnight sensations. What we often learn when we dig deeper is that those performers spent years practicing their craft, performing in numerous small venues around the country, or took years of classes in order to practice and perfect their skills.

Like performers learning their craft, you are learning how to live with your loss. Things take time. Your grief won't disappear just because you want it to. In fact, it may come and go for a long time. That is its natural process.

Your Unique Grief

*I measure every Grief I meet
With narrow, probing, Eyes—
I wonder if It weighs like Mine—
Or has an Easier size.*

—Emily Dickinson, American poet

Sometimes the biggest obstacle in getting through a loss is not the loss itself, but our notion of how we should react to it. We feel that we should be sad; we should feel remorse; we should be upset. In truth, there is no right or wrong way to deal with loss, nor how long the mourning period should last, nor what stages of the grieving process we will or will not experience.

Some people think that grief lasts a year. They wonder why they are still grieving after that time. Grief has its own timetable. Just as one person is totally different from another, so too is one person's grieving process different from anyone else's.

The same is true of the intensity of grief. Some people experience a loss and move on shortly afterward. For others, it takes a much longer time.

And, even though such things as anger, depression, guilt, numbness, being overwhelmed, and shock are part of grief, you may experience all of them, some of them, or none of them.

Try not to compare your grief to someone else's. You are unique.

So is your grief.

When You Least Expect Them

*Tears are the safety valve of the heart
when too much pressure is laid on it.*

–Albert Smith, author (attributed)

Some days, after my wife died, I would wake up in the morning feeling pretty good. I thought my tears were over. Then they would start again when I least expected it.

For example, on my way to work some days, whenever I walked past the Bank of America building in downtown San Francisco, I would burst out crying. I don't know why I did. I just did. I had no idea why it happened at that particular spot. Was it the massiveness and the darkness of the structure? I will never know.

What I do know is that grief, and the tears that it can trigger, can rear its head at the most unusual moment. Tears are a natural part of the grieving process, but you can't plan when they will happen. They seem to have a mind of their own. They might start while dining in a restaurant with friends, during a meeting at work, or while traveling on public transportation.

Don't hold back the tears. Let them flow.

Setbacks Are Normal

All the world is full of suffering.
It is also full of overcoming.

–Helen Keller, deaf/blind American author

What I found after my wife died was that setbacks were part of the normal grieving and healing process. Some days would feel like I had finally put my loss behind me. Other days the loss seemed overwhelming.

You too may feel, on some days, that you have taken one step forward and two backward. Accept those days. It may not seem so now, but down the road, there is a good chance that you will take three steps forward and none back.

Your world right now may feel like it is filled with suffering. What you may not be able to see right now is that it can also filled with overcoming.

You Are Not Alone

*One word or a pleasing smile is often enough
to raise up a saddened and wounded soul.*

–Therese of Lisieux, Catholic saint

When I was about seven years old, my parents took me to
see the musical *Carousel* on Broadway. I still remember one
haunting song in that show. It is "You'll Never Walk Alone."
In the show, the song is sung to give Julie Jordan, one of the
leading characters, strength and courage after the father of her
child, Billy Bigelow, is killed.

The lyrics talk about holding your head up high, not being
afraid of the dark, and finding a golden sky at the end of
the storm. They gave me comfort and courage during many
difficult times in my life. It may do the same for you. Seek it
out and listen to it, if you can. Or, find another song, poem,
quotation, book, prayer, or grief support group to remind you
that you are not alone in your loss.

It may feel like you are the only one to ever experience such an
intense loss, but you are not. Others have gotten through their
loss and they have survived. You can too.

Pat Yourself on the Back

*Whenever you feel uncomfortable, instead of
retreating back into your old comfort zone,
pat yourself on the back and say, "I must be
growing," and continue moving forward.*

–T. Harv Eker, motivational speaker/author

When we accidentally stub our toe or nick one of our fingers, we often shout out, "Ouch!" Grieving is the body's way of saying "ouch" after a loss. It is telling us to stop what we are doing, take some time off, and admit that loss hurts.

Dealing with a loss is not easy. You have been going through a lot. In fact, it might be the hardest thing you have ever done in your life. Perhaps it is time to acknowledge that under the circumstances, you are doing the best you can right now.

So, reach one arm over your shoulder and give yourself a great big pat on the back.

Additional Thoughts on Losing

Should you shield the canyons from the windstorms,
you would never see the true beauty of their carvings

–Elisabeth Kübler-Ross, Swiss-born psychiatrist

We must embrace pain and burn
it as fuel for our journey.

–Kenji Miyazawa, Japanese poet

The lights of stars that were extinguished
ages ago still reach us. So it is with great men
who died centuries ago, but still reach us
with the radiation of their personalities.

–Kahlil Gibran, poet

Step Two

Learning

> *Turn your wounds into wisdom.*
>
> **—Oprah Winfrey, American television host**

Every time you lose something, you are presented with an opportunity to acquire something new. With each loss, there is a golden opportunity for a new beginning. You may not realize it right now, but your loss is part of your growth process. In fact, your loss can be seen as a gift.

How could you possibly even think of loss as a gift? You have lost someone who was very dear to you. You have perhaps lost the one person in your life who meant everything to you. You have lost a significant part of who you were. It certainly doesn't feel like a gift.

And yet, it is.

Your loss is serving you. It is helping you examine who you are, why you are on this earth, and how to live your life. Among other things, your loss has given you:

- the gift of appreciating life more fully
- the gift of cleansing through mourning

- the gift of love

The best thing you can do after reading this is to open the gift.

The Seasons

In the depth of winter, I finally learned that
within me there lay an invincible summer.

–Albert Camus, French writer

You may feel that you are in the midst of the coldest, darkest winter of your life. But think of the seasons. In nature, after winter comes spring and then summer always follows.

You too are part of nature. Your loss has created the season of winter. But somewhere inside of you there is also the new growth of spring and the warmth of summer waiting to emerge.

Inner Strength

*I…walked for miles at night along the beach, writing
bad blank verse and searching endlessly for someone
wonderful who would…change my life.
It never crossed my mind that that person could be me.*

—Anna Quindlen, American author

I am male.

I am seventy-two years old.

I am bald.

I have a beard.

I grew up in the Bronx.

I now live in San Francisco.

I am married.

I have one daughter.

I have one brother.

I like herbal tea, poppyseed strudel, and kosher pickles.

I have a Master of Fine Arts degree.

I am a professional speaker.

I am an author.

The above list tells you a little about me. But it doesn't really tell you one of the most important things. It doesn't tell you that I am a survivor. It doesn't tell you that I have survived many losses in my life.

None of those losses, however, make me unique. We are all survivors, including you. There is a good chance that if you are alive, you have experienced the loss of people you knew or someone you loved.

Losing is part of living.

It is also part of learning.

Losing teaches you that life goes on and that you can too.

Each loss also teaches you about your inner strengths that you probably never knew you had. Now is the time to tap into them.

Take Courage

*Pain nourishes courage. You can't be brave if you've
only had wonderful things happen to you.*

—Mary Tyler Moore, American actress

Life is filled with trials and tribulations. They are often painful
and unwanted. There is no way of avoiding them.

Still, as annoying and agonizing as they are, without those
ordeals, your life would be shallow. They help mold you into
who you are and bolster your courage. They help you grow as
a person and increase your compassion for others who might
also be in pain.

In loss, you also learn that, if you can overcome your present
ordeal, you have the courage within you to survive future
losses as well.

Remembering Those Who Left Us

Think about someone who you've lost and write down the ways that person positively affected your life. How is your life better today for having known him or her?

–Julie Clark Robinson, American author

If you have lost a loved one or a close friend, the hardest time in the grieving process is often around the holidays. And, although it may be a bitter time without them, you can sweeten those times with their loving memories.

A few things you can do, holidays or not, are:

- Recall a good-time story about them. Tell it to others.

- Cook one of their favorite foods. Share it with friends.

- Go through photo albums. Display a couple of your favorites.

In addition, think about how your loved ones would want you to remember them. Would they want you to be somber and solemn for the rest of your life, or would they want you to celebrate their lives by remembering the happier times you spent together?

For most of us, it would be to honor the latter.

Still Here

*If you're connected to someone in a moment
of love, the essence of that person is right
there with you even after their death.*

–Ram Dass, spiritual teacher

Shortly after my wife died, I tapped into her great sense of
humor and started to do workshops on the therapeutic value
of humor and laughter. In one of my very first presentations,
I was shocked when I looked around the room. There, in the
back row, was a woman who looked exactly like my deceased
wife. I was taken aback and made a mental note to speak to
her at the break. When the break came, I started to make my
way to the corner where the woman was seated, but someone
interrupted me to ask a question. By the time I got to the rear
of the room, the woman was gone. And she never returned for
the second half of the program. Was that woman really there?
Was I only imagining it? Was it my wife's spirit in the room?

I took the incident as a sign from my wife. She was letting me
know that she was okay—that she was watching over me, and
that I was on the right path.

You may have lost someone you loved very much. While it is
true that the physical body is no longer here, the spirit still is.

Perhaps not as dramatically as I had experienced, but the spirit of the person you lost will always be with you. It will guide and encourage you.

Know that they are there for you whenever you need their support.

Twenty-One Grams

I know you're there
Although it's nothing I can prove
I know you're there
From just the way the shadows move
And though I said goodbye and fin'ly let you go
I know you're there
Although I don't know how I know.

—Alix Korey, American composer

In 1907, researcher Duncan MacDougall found that twenty-one grams of body weight were lost immediately after a person died. He interpreted the weight loss as a sign of the soul leaving the body. The tests were never replicated, and the results were widely dismissed by the scientific community. Still, it does bring up the question of what, if anything, remains when we die.

We may never be able to prove that the soul or spirit exists or whether it leaves the body upon death. But what we can be certain of is a lingering memory of those who have gone before us. And that, if nothing else, is the true soul or spirit of a living being.

It is that spirit of the deceased that we carry around with us in our thoughts. It is those memories that keep that person's essence alive. And, when we think or speak of that person, though the body may not be around anymore, that person's spirit continues forever.

Larger Than Your Loss

Adversity has the effect of eliciting talents which, in prosperous circumstances, would have lain dormant.

—Horace, Roman poet

When my wife died at the age of thirty-four, I thought my life had ended.

How could I go on living without her?

How was I going to raise my young daughter alone?

What was I going to do with my life now?

What I didn't realize at the time, and what I couldn't possibly know then, was that in the bigger picture, my wife's death was an important part of my life's intricate plan. She was here to lay the foundation for both me and my daughter and our own unique contributions to the betterment of the world, as well as to enrich our spiritual paths.

You are larger than your loss, which is why you will be able to survive it. And, paradoxically, your loss is larger than you, which is why it will teach you more than you ever imagined.

Becoming Bigger

*Life is a series of experiences, each of which makes
us bigger, even though it is hard to realize this.
For the world was built to develop character, and
we must learn that the setbacks and grieves which
we endure help us in our marching onward.*

—Henry Ford, American industrialist

No matter how horrendous the loss you have experienced is,
no matter how devastated you may be right now, you are bigger
than your loss. You are stronger than your loss.

Right now, in the midst of your loss, you probably don't feel
very strong. Someday, however, you may look back and see
how this loss has given you emotional and mental qualities you
never realized you had.

Loss makes us larger. It helps us discover a force we had inside
of us that perhaps we never knew we had. It gives us eyes to
see new things and ears to listen to the world in new ways. It
awakens our senses and helps us to realize the preciousness
and incredible magnificence of life.

With a Little Help from Your Friends

> You think your pains and heartbreaks are
> unprecedented in the history of the world, but
> then you read. It was books that taught me that
> the things that tormented me were the very
> things that connected me with all the people
> who were alive, or who have ever been alive.

—James Baldwin, American author

The Romani people know that support is important in critical times. When a member of the community gets sick, a group of family members and friends accompany the person who is ill to the doctor.

Take a lesson from the Romani. Get help. Join a grief support group.

These groups were created to help you deal with your loss. Take advantage of them. They are there to support you. They will help you in your recovery process and help you realize that, in time, you will heal.

Being in a support group will also show you that you are not alone. You will see others who have gone through some of the same things you are going through. You will also see that they have successfully gotten through their loss.

And, with the shared tears and laughter of a group, you see that it is possible to live and even laugh again.

Connect With Others

*A real friend is the one who walks in when
the rest of the world walks out.*

—Walter Winchell (attributed)

In addition to a support group, you might also look for
someone special who you know would bring the greatest
comfort during your time of loss.

There were two of those people in my life when my wife died.
One was a volunteer at a grief center and the other was my
young daughter. The volunteer and I would meet once a week.
She didn't offer advice on how I should overcome my grief.
She simply told me her story of loss and I told her mine. We
chatted; we laughed; we cried. We consoled and comforted
each other.

The other person was my ten-year-old daughter. Yes, I had the
support of friends and family members, and yes, I even went
to a therapist, but the biggest help was that of my young child.
She was open, she was direct, and she gave me hope to go on
when all else was seemingly lost.

Who is it that can sit with you, give you a hug, and be the
shoulder you can cry on?

The Power of Hope

It's never the end of the world.
It's already tomorrow in Australia.

—Charles M. Schulz, American cartoonist

During your loss, you may have been so angry or despondent that you blurted out a number of curse words, including some four-letter ones. But there is another four-letter word that might serve you better at this time. That word is "hope."

Hope is the greatest treasure you have.

When all else fails, hope is something to hang onto.

Don't give up.

The Highest Good

Higher Good is like water. It benefits us all.

–The Tao Te Ching

When I grew up, we lived in a very Jewish neighborhood in the Bronx. If we went out to dinner, it would always be to the same Chinese restaurant. And we would order the same exact thing each week: one dish from column A and two dishes from column B.

In those days, from my limited perspective, I thought that everyone in the world was Jewish and that everyone ate at a Chinese restaurant on Sunday. It wasn't until I attended an out-of-town school and met people from all over the world that I realized that not everyone lived as I did.

Like my Bronx upbringing, our view of the universe is very limited. We cannot see beyond our lifespan. Thus, we cannot always see what is best for the universe as a whole.

The best we can do, therefore, is ask that what is happening to us—even if it be a major loss in our life—is for the highest good.

What's Empty, Fills

Nature abhors a vacuum.

–H. Emilie Cady, American physician/author

Sit quietly and try to empty your mind of any thoughts. For a few minutes, see if you can not think of anything at all. You will probably find this very difficult to do, maybe near impossible. You might be able to do this for a few seconds or so, but chances are that as soon as one thought leaves, another rushes in to fill it.

Nature is like that too. Lift a rock in a river and water will immediately flow into the crevice and fill it up again. Like the void created by removing the rock in the river, something has been removed in your life and has created an empty space. Know that the emptiness is only temporary. Things cannot remain empty forever. When there is an empty space, it gets filled up again with something else. That is a law of nature.

There is a space in your life right now. Take comfort in knowing that in time, it will be refilled. You may not yet know with what, or when, but it will.

Opportunity Knocks

*After pain is always a new opportunity. You can
count on it, like the day following the night.*

–Anthony Robbins, American self-help author/speaker

I grew up in New York City. So, I never really needed a car,
owned one, or learned to drive. When my wife and I moved
to San Francisco, she was the designated driver of the car we
bought. When she died, the car sat in the driveway for six
months. I would look at it every day and finally realized that I
had to make a decision about it.

I could sell it. I could let it rust there. Or, I could learn to drive.
I chose the latter.

Little did I realize at the time I learned to drive that I could
never do the work I am currently doing—traveling around the
country giving presentations on therapeutic humor—without
having my driver's license. One part of my life ended with my
loss, but another began.

Now that one part of your life has ended, another will begin.

Be patient.

Seeds of the Best

The worst thing in your life may contain seeds of the best. When you can see crisis as an opportunity your life becomes not easier, but more satisfying.

—Joe Kogel, American humorist

My wife's death allowed me to see things that I hadn't noticed before. It forced me to look inward to see my own finitude, my own beauty, and the beauty in others. Once I started to accept her death, my life opened up and became fuller and richer. Material things had less meaning for me, and my spiritual and inner growth became more important to me.

Perhaps, as the quotation above states, you can see your loss—"the worst thing in your life"—containing some seeds of the best. If you are having trouble doing that, consider the oyster. It takes an irritating piece of sand within its body and creates a glowing, radiant pearl.

What positive thing might come out of your loss?

Living and Losing

*Life does not accommodate you, it shatters you. It
is meant to and it couldn't do it better. Every seed
destroys its container or else there would be no fruition.*

–Florida Scott-Maxwell, American author

If you are alive, you will experience some loss in your life. That
is the law of nature.

Think of a tree. In the fall, the leaves drop to the ground. In the
winter, they decay and provide nourishment for the tree. In the
spring, the tree blooms again—fuller, richer, and more radiant
than before, because those fallen leaves fed it.

You are not much different than a tree.

The people you have lost are part of life's cycle. They live, they
die, and they nurture those that come after them. You are one
of those people. Be thankful that they have been in your life.

Finding Meaning in Your Loss

*I know that they are in heaven…and I know that
that's why this movement is growing because we
have tens of thousands of angels behind us that are
supporting us, that are saying, "Well, you know we
died and that was really crappy, but we hope that
our deaths are going to make the world a better
place," and it's up to us to make sure that it does.*

–Cindy Sheehan, American anti-war activist

In his book *Man's Search for Meaning*, Viktor Frankl relates a
story about an elderly man who grieved for two years over the
death of his wife. Frankl asked the man, "What would have
happened if you had died first, and your wife would have had
to survive you?" The man answered, "Oh, for her this would
have been terrible; how she would have suffered!" Frankl
responded, "You see…such a suffering has been spared to her,
and it was you who have spared her this suffering—to be sure,
at the price that now you have to survive and mourn her."

Frankl observed, "In some way, suffering ceases to be suffering
at the moment it finds a meaning."

What has happened to you has happened. You can't change that. But you can change what you do with it. Can you find some meaning in your loss?

Keeping Your Loved One Alive

When we die, we die three times. First, when
our brain ceases to function. Second, when
our heart stops beating. Third, when our
name is no longer spoken in the world.

—Jewish saying

My daughter was ten years old when my wife died. The three years that we knew my wife had a terminal illness were a terrible strain on both of us. I realized after my wife's death that my daughter and I needed a reprieve from what we had been through; we needed an adventure. So I booked a trip to Alaska on the Inside Passage ferry system. And what an adventure it was. We went whitewater rafting, took seaplane rides, and spent the night next to a calving glacier.

Taking the trip was an instinctual decision but, looking back, a very wise one. It not only helped take our minds off of our loss, but it also helped us bond. That bonding allowed us to talk openly about Ellen's death. It made it easier to not hide our feelings or avoid conversations about our loss. It also allowed us to both laugh and cry together.

We would often talk about missing Ellen. Frequently, when we didn't quite know what to do in a situation, we would turn to each other and ask, "What would Mommy do?" And then do it her way. Often, we discussed Ellen as if she were alive and still part of our life, which, on some level, she was. And we continued to have those conversations, although less so as time went on.

To keep your loved one alive, learn from the lessons they have left for you and you will be speaking of them often.

Wake-Up Call

Most people don't know there are angels whose only job is to make sure you don't get too comfortable and fall asleep and miss your life.

—Brian Andreas, founder of StoryPeople

In Thornton Wilder's play *Our Town*, a young woman named Emily dies and goes to heaven. On her first day there, she wants to return to earth for just one more day. She is granted her wish and is taken back in time. Home again, she notices that her family fails to appreciate the simple magnificence of life: the sunflowers, the food, the coffee, the newly ironed dresses, the hot baths, and sleeping and waking up. "Do any human beings," Emily poignantly asks, "ever realize life while they live it?"

Your loss may seem more like a curse now than a blessing, but someday you may understand why those you have lost were a godsend. Those angels in disguise provided you with a wake-up call to appreciate the little things in life, for it is those little things that life is really all about.

Closer to Your Core

The most intense moments in our life, like losing someone very close to us, can bring us closer to our core. Because death is such a powerful force, it awakens some fire in us and connects us to the deceased and the world around us.

—Judy Tatelbaum, American author/therapist

After my wife died, I sold the silk screening business I had. I knew that there was something else I was supposed to do in my life. I didn't know what that was, but silk screening was not it. So I got rid of the business and hung out for a while, waiting to see what the universe would bring. Not long after, a catalog from the Holistic Life University came in the mail. One of the tracks they taught was about death and dying. I enrolled in the program, became the director of it several years later, and began my new journey.

I had no idea where any of this would take me, but I followed my gut. I gave up the business I owned, went down a new path, and followed my desire to teach people about the therapeutic value of humor. All this stemmed from a loss that brought me closer to my core and led me to my passion.

Be open to where your loss might lead you.

A New World

When we are no longer able to change a situation...
we are challenged to change ourselves.

—Viktor Frankl, Austrian psychiatrist

Loss instantly changes your world. The once-familiar becomes strange. But, with time, the strange will become familiar.

The loss of someone you loved puts you in a whole new world—a world of living without them. It takes a lot of adjusting to get used to this new world and to move forward in it. Moving forward, however, does not imply forgetting those who are no longer with you. It just means that you will be leaving one chapter of your life behind you and moving on to the next one.

Like the chapters in a book, we know what was in the preceding chapter, but we don't know what is to come. That's what makes books so interesting.

Not knowing what comes next can make life interesting too.

Embrace Change

Don't judge change as being either good or bad.
Just let it happen. One and the same thing can at
the same time be good, bad, and indifferent, e.g.,
music is good to the melancholy, bad to those who
mourn, and neither good or bad to the deaf.

–Baruch Spinoza, Dutch philosopher

While change may be unsettling, it is what every living thing is about. Everything changes, even the vast oceans of the world. Every day, their tides rise and fall dramatically.

I have learned a lot about change from a large ornamental plum tree outside my kitchen window. It is constantly changing. In winter, it has no leaves. In spring, it has beautiful flowers. In summer, it has a small supply of plums. And in the fall, the leaves begin to drop as it starts its changing process all over again.

In her book *The First 30 Days*, author Ariane de Bonvoisin has a "Change Manifesto." Although she is writing about change in general, some of her suggestions are very relevant to dealing with change that occurs after a loss. Among them are:

- Change is part of life and happens to everyone.

- Change brings new people, new opportunities, and new perspectives.

- Change helps me strengthen my self-reliance, inner fortitude, and inner faith that I can handle anything.

- Change is never punishment; it is always an opportunity to connect with what's inside me.

- Change reminds me that I am not in control of many things that happen and reminds me to let go and to surrender a little more to life.

- Change helps me find my highest self—the part of me that is always there, that doesn't change. Life's unpredictability becomes infinitely easier when I connect with that part of myself.

- Change is always on my side. It exists to serve me, teach me lessons, and help me embrace life's mysteries.

The Human Spirit

*Man has never made any material as
resilient as the human spirit.*

–Bernard Williams, English philosopher

Your spirit may be down. Your spirit may feel like it is broken.
That is only temporary.

Get up again.

Once you do, your spirit will begin to mend. Someday, your
spirit will be whole again.

Additional Thoughts on Learning

We cannot live the afternoon of life according to the program of life's morning, for what was great in the morning will be little at evening and what in the morning was true, at evening will have become a lie.

–Carl Gustav Jung, Swiss psychiatrist

Sometimes, in the winds of change, we find our direction.

–Anonymous

When you have something like heart surgery, you appreciate the simple things, like breathing.

–Robin Williams, American comedian

Step Three

Letting Go

> *The longer we dwell on our misfortunes,*
> *the greater is their power to harm us.*
>
> **—Voltaire, French philosopher**

Crying is the body's way of dealing with loss. It is unhealthy to squelch your tears. What you stifle today may come back in greater force tomorrow. But continuing to endlessly wallow in those tears is not healthy. At some point, you need to get on with your life.

Today might be the day to take the first step, to let go, to move on.

Things Are Different Now

*The pessimist complains about the wind; the optimist
expects it to change; the realist adjusts the sails.*

–William Arthur Ward, American author

After your loss, things will be different. That doesn't mean they
have to be bad.

How you view what has happened to you depends on whether
you are a pessimist, an optimist, or a realist.

The wind has changed.

It may be time to adjust your sails.

Bend Without Breaking

As I started to picture the trees in the storm, the answer began to dawn on me. The trees in the storm don't try to stand up straight and tall and erect. They allow themselves to bend and be blown with the wind. They understand the power of letting go. Those trees and those branches that try too hard to stand up strong and straight are the ones that break.

–Julia Butterfly Hill, American environmentalist

While writing this book, a friend, who was also a distant relative, passed away. It wasn't unexpected, since he had been under hospice care for the past few weeks. But it still hurt. It upset me even more because I already had airline tickets and was planning on visiting with him during my trip to New York City. But he had gone before I could get there. His death forced me to let go of my plans and expectations.

The incident made me realize how often in life we have to let go. For example, at home, our youngsters leave the house for the first time and go off to kindergarten or camp. Let go. Then they go off to college. Let go. Then they get married and permanently move away. Let go.

Then there is the world at work. You don't get the job or the raise you want. Let go. You are transferred to a new city. Let go. The boss you really like retires. Let go. Or, you retire and no longer have the job you had been doing for perhaps the past thirty to forty years. Let go.

Then there is aging. You can't walk as far or as fast as you once did. Let go. You can't see or hear as well as you did previously. Let go.

And, finally, there is death—perhaps the ultimate letting go. Let go.

This Too Shall Pass

The past cannot be changed.
The future is still in your power.

—Hugh White, American politician

Right now, you may feel that there is nothing to live for. But remember, as with everything else in life, nothing stays the same. Everything changes.

And this too shall pass.

Change Is Inevitable

The only person who likes change is a wet baby.

—Roy Blitzer, management consultant

Many years ago, I went to see the movie *Groundhog Day*. When the film was over, I took the elevator to the lobby of the theater complex. In the elevator, two young teenage boys were talking about the film. One said to the other, "I hated the movie. Nothing happens."

And, if you know the film, the teenagers are right. Bill Murray's character finds himself repeating the same day over and over again. When he gets up each morning, the same song is playing on the radio, the same overnight blizzard has blanketed the area, and the same people are on the same street in the exact same place doing and saying the exact same things they did the day before.

The movie is a great example of what would probably happen if things never changed. Like the Murray character, you would be so totally bored that you would probably start to go nuts. Change is what makes life challenging and exciting.

Change happens. It is inevitable. And it is needed. Sometimes we like it when things change. Sometimes, as in loss, we don't. But there is really not much we can do about it, except let go.

Losing and Choosing

*Everything can be taken from a man but
one thing: the last of the human freedoms—
to choose one's attitude in any given set of
circumstances, to choose one's own way.*

—Viktor Frankl, Austrian psychiatrist/Holocaust survivor

In one of my workshops, I asked a woman (a volunteer director
at a local hospital) what stressed her out the most. She said
that it was when volunteers don't show up. I tried to give her
some techniques to let go of this stressful situation, but she
refused to even consider these. The more I suggested ways
to lighten up the situation, the more she held onto her upset,
and, because of her continued stubbornness, the more the
audience laughed.

Letting go is not easy, particularly after a loss. But, like the
woman above, you have a choice. You can let your grief engulf
your life, or you can choose to begin to embrace life again.

Forgiving Others

*One of the greatest struggles of the healing process
is to forgive both yourself and others and to stop
expending valuable energy on the past hurts.*

—Caroline Myss, American author

Before you can fully embrace life again, you need to let go of any anger you have toward the person you lost. Carrying around that upset only gets in the way of truly experiencing life. That anger is like a stranglehold that person still has on you, even though that person may no longer be around.

Forgive the deceased:

- for wanting more than you might have been capable of giving

- for something they may have done or said that upset you

- for leaving you

And remember, even though your loved ones are no longer around, you can still forgive them. It is not really for them anyway; it is for you.

In addition to forgiving the deceased, you may also want to forgive others who were involved in the loss too.

Forgive:

- the doctor who wasn't able to save your loved one
- a friend or relative who wasn't there for you
- anyone who can't sympathize with your loss

Forgiving Yourself

Forgiveness is a funny thing.
It warms the heart and cools the sting.

–William Arthur Ward, American author

If you want to let go and move on with your life, you need to not only forgive other people who may have hurt or disappointed you, but you also have to forgive yourself.

Forgive yourself:

- for things you wanted to say to the deceased but did not

- for not being able to bring back your loved one

- for any guilt you are having now that they are gone

Healing begins to happen when you can forgive yourself.

Keep On Forgiving

Forgiveness does not change the past,
but it does enlarge the future.

–Paul Boese, Dutch botanist

When dealing with a loss, people try to be helpful. Sometimes, however, they say the wrong thing and are more hurtful than helpful. If someone makes you angry by saying things like, "It's probably for the best," "Don't take it so hard," or "Life is difficult," realize that people sometimes have a hard time being around death and dying situations. They mean well but don't always know the most comforting thing to say or do.

Forgive them too.

Ask Others for Forgiveness

> *He that cannot forgive others breaks the*
> *bridge over which he must pass himself;*
> *for everyman has need to be forgiven.*

—Edward Herbert, British diplomat

Just as we must forgive ourselves and others, in order to move on, it is important to ask for forgiveness from others. Dealing with a loss can be all-consuming. While you were in the midst of that turmoil, were you:

- curt with someone who was trying to help?

- forgetting to thank people for their support?

- not communicating well with friends and family?

Ask them to forgive you.

Do you also need to ask forgiveness from the deceased:

- for not doing more to help them?

- for not being as compassionate as they wanted you to be?

- for not being able to save them?

Ask them to forgive you too.

Inner Peace

Take a leap in faith and trust in love, trust God.
Choose to experience peace rather than conflict.
Choose to experience love rather than fear and
guilt. Choose to be a love finder rather than a fault
finder. Choose to be a love giver rather than a love
seeker. Teach only love for that is what you are.

—Gerald Jampolsky, American psychiatrist

Once you have forgiven other people as well as the person
you have lost, and yourself, you will begin to experience inner
peace. It is from that place that you can now let go and allow
the joy of life to once again enter your world.

Look Within

I shut my eyes in order to see.

–Paul Gauguin, French artist

Sometimes, when someone dies, there is so much commotion among family members and friends that it is hard to think clearly. Those people mean well, but you may need a little time for yourself.

Sit quietly for a while with your thoughts and your feelings.

In a somewhat playful manner, Martin Boroson, author of *One-Moment Meditation*, suggests a very simple, very short way to look inside in order to, as he calls it, "refresh your browser."

Close your eyes and shift your focus from what you were looking at to what you can hear.

As you listen to the sounds around you, without judging them or even identifying them, breathe deeply.

Then open your eyes and shift your focus back to what you can see...now with fresh eyes.

You have refreshed your browser.

Remember to Breathe

Breathe. Let go. And remind yourself that this very moment is the only one you know you have for sure.

—Oprah Winfrey, American television host

It may sound silly to remind you to breathe, since breathing is such a natural state. But when you are under stress, your breaths become shallow. You tighten up and forget just how calming slow, deep breathing can be.

Some simple breathing-related phrases might remind you to keep taking slow, deep breaths:

- to get one's breath back

- to breathe freely again

- to breathe confidently

- to breathe new life into something

- to breathe a sigh of relief

Now, take a slow, deep breath and let go.

Let Go of the Past

You can clutch the past so tightly to your chest that it leaves your arms too full to embrace the present.

–Jan Glidewell, American columnist

What has happened in the past has happened. There is absolutely nothing you can do to bring your loved one back.

But you can let go of the past, live in the present, and be hopeful about the future.

Rejoice in a Life Lived

> *When a child is born, all rejoice; when someone*
> *dies, all weep. But it makes just as much sense,*
> *if not more, to rejoice at the end of a life as at*
> *the beginning. For no one can tell what events*
> *await a newborn child, but when a mortal dies*
> *he has successfully completed a journey.*

—The Talmud

Right now, you may be mourning for a life lost. But you can also celebrate that life lived.

Celebrate the good times you had together.

Celebrate how the deceased enriched your world.

Celebrate the wonderful things that person meant to you.

And remember, it doesn't matter how long that loved one's life was. Like a beautiful symphony, it is the beauty of the music that matters—not the length of the piece.

Trust Your Gut

*Follow your instincts. That's where
true wisdom manifests itself.*

–Oprah Winfrey, American television host

"When a train goes through a tunnel and it gets dark," wrote Holocaust survivor Corrie ten Boom, "you don't throw away the ticket and jump off. You sit still and trust the engineer."

You may feel that you are in a dark tunnel right now. But tunnels don't go on forever. At some point, they end. As the old cliché says, there is always light at the end of the tunnel.

At some point in your despair, you will realize that you cannot stay in this dark place forever. Something inside of you will tell you that it is time to move on.

Listen to that inner voice.

Additional Thoughts On Letting Go

*Hanging onto resentment is letting someone
you despise live rent-free in your head.*

–Ann Landers, American syndicated columnist

*Whatever you think people are withholding
from you–give it to them…Soon after you
start giving, you will start receiving.*

–Eckhart Tolle, German spiritual teacher

When I let go of what I am, I become what I might be.

–Lao Tzu, Chinese philosopher

Step Four

Living

> *I can choose to sit in perpetual sadness,*
> *immobilized by the gravity of my loss, or I*
> *can choose to rise from the pain and treasure*
> *the most precious gift I have—life itself.*
>
> **–Walter Anderson, American magazine editor**

The loss of someone close to you provides an opportunity for a new beginning and an enriched life. Once you start to work through your grief process, you can begin to fill the vacuum that was created by your loss with an even fuller sense of life.

Ultimately, in dealing with a loss, the choice is yours. No matter what the situation, you have a choice of how you react to it. You can remain in your grief and turn your face away from life, or you can move on and embrace it.

Choose life.

Getting On With Life

Being fully alive to life is truly a heroic act. Many of us think heroism means rescuing people from burning buildings or being daring in wartime. Instead, heroism is an everyday affair. For some of us, getting up in the morning and facing another day is a heroic act. For others, changing jobs, losing jobs, or living with health problems, or staying in a relationship or managing on limited funds or facing the loss of a loved one is a heroic act. We have many opportunities to be heroes in our daily lives. The heroism of which I speak is the courage to be fully alive to life, regardless of our circumstances.

—Judy Tatelbaum, American author/therapist

Sometimes after a loss, it feels like you too are in the land of the dead. At some point, you need to move to the land of the living and get on with your life.

Sitting around bemoaning your loss only gets you deeper into a downward spiral. At some point, no matter how hard it might be, if you are to heal from your loss, you must do something other than wallow in it. You must start living again.

If you don't, you will have created a double loss—the person who has died and the loss of your own spirit.

To Live Again

*The person who removes a mountain
begins by carrying away small stones.*

–Chinese proverb

Sometimes the first step is the hardest.

But, remember, without that first step, there is no second.

To fully live life again, take the first step.

Take Back Your Life

When we hate our enemies, we are giving them power over us: power over our sleep, our appetites, our blood pressure, our health and our happiness. Our enemies would dance with joy if only they knew how they were worrying us, lacerating us, and getting even with us! Our hate is not hurting them at all, but our hate is turning our days and nights into a hellish turmoil.

—Dale Carnegie, American writer

You may feel that your life has been robbed. Something very precious has been taken away from you. That may be true. Yet one simple uplifting thought can change that feeling.

A letter I received from a woman who found an inspiring quotation in one of my books showed me how the power of just a few words can help overcome a terrible incident. The woman wrote:

> At the age of twelve, I was violently raped twice. I have never told anyone, but it haunted me for fifty-five years. It affected me in every aspect of my life. I was constantly filled with anger and rage. In reading your book, one phrase stood out, "When we hate our enemies, we give them power over us. Our sleep, our health..." Because

of that quotation, I have taken my power back and it has changed my life.

Can you find a quotation, a phrase, a song, a prayer, or a poem that will help you take back your life?

It Takes Effort

To think bad thoughts is really the easiest thing in the world. If you leave your mind to itself, it will spiral down into ever increasing unhappiness.
To think good thoughts, however, requires effort.

–James Clavell, British/American novelist

Some days it may take all the effort you have to get out of bed.

Make the effort.

Some days it takes effort just to smile.

Smile anyway.

Some days it may be difficult to find one thing to be happy about.

Keep seeking.

Pulling yourself out of your loss may take effort. But it is worth it. You are worth it. Make the effort.

Keep Moving

*Life leaps like a geyser for those who
drill through the rock of inertia.*

–Alexis Carrel, French physician

A friend and colleague of mine, Carl Hammerschlag, told me a
wonderful story about the key to living life fully:

> I was in New York's Metropolitan Museum of Art when an
> old woman comes up to me and says, "Excuse me, young
> man. Can you tell me what time it is?" I look at my watch
> and say, "It's exactly two o'clock." She tells me that she had
> a two o'clock appointment with friends, but they aren't
> here. Then, she continues on, without a comma or period,
> that she was rarely late for appointments, knew nothing
> about primitive art, worked at the Bronx Botanical
> Gardens. I'm daydreaming, looking at her, five-foot-two,
> neatly dressed in a blue suit with a matching pillbox hat.
> In her white-gloved hand, she is carrying a handbag.
> Politely trying to get away, I hear her say, "That's the secret
> of life." I know I've missed something, so I ask her, "What's
> the secret of life?" And she says, "Sneakers are the secret of
> life." I have no idea what she is talking about, but as I look
> down more carefully, I see that accompanying her Easter

ensemble, she is wearing sneakers. I know I've missed something again, so I ask her, "How are sneakers the secret of life?" And she repeats, "I wear these sneakers because they are only comfortable when you keep moving. That's the secret of life; you gotta keep moving."

So now that you know the secret of life, put on your sneakers and keep moving.

Get Out of the House

A ship is safe in harbor,
but that's not what ships are for.

–William Shedd, American Presbyterian theologian

While cleaning out my closet, I found a jar that contained some seashells I had found on a beach many years ago. They had attractive shapes and colors, but I remember how much more brilliant they were when I first found them on the beach. In the jar, they were still pretty, but they lost their luster; they didn't have the glow they once had.

When you are dealing with a loss, becoming a hermit in your residence may seem like an easy way out. You don't have to deal with an unsympathetic world. It feels comfortable. It is safe.

However, staying at home—particularly if you lived in the same household with the deceased—you are constantly surrounded by memories of that person. It will only bring you down. If you wait for your grief to completely go away, which it rarely does, you will never do anything.

Get out of the house. Have lunch with friends. Go to a movie or a museum. Nothing happens when you stay at home.

Like those shells in the jar, you need to get away from your container in order to regain your luster and lust for life.

As scary as it seems, you must get out of the house.

Do It Anyway

Life is risky; we are all acrobats tiptoeing over one bridge or another. To a tightrope walker the rope is just like home. Those who hold their bodies lightly and their minds simply may seem in danger, but they are safe.

–Chinese scroll saying

Recently I received an email from a woman who lost her young husband in a car crash. She said that with his death, her "life has not been and never will be the same."

And she is right. It never will be the same. But that does not mean that her life, or yours after your loss, cannot be fulfilling.

One of the things that death teaches us is that life is short; if you want to do something, you probably should not put it off, or you may never get to do it. Death also teaches us that life is filled with risks and that we need to take some of those risks if we are to reap life's rewards.

After my wife died, I realized it was time to confront some of those risks and do things I had been putting off for years. I learned to drive a car for the first time at the age of forty-two. I went back to school to get my master's degree. I gave up a business I co-owned and started a new one.

In spite of your loss and the feeling that your life may never be the same, the death of a loved one can bring a surprisingly new life. I encourage you to seek yours.

What small risk can you take today that might help you live fully again?

Do Something New

*I have always been delighted at the prospect of a
new day, a fresh try, one more start, with perhaps a bit
of magic waiting somewhere behind the morning.*

—J. B. Priestly, English author

One of the things that can happen when you are dealing with a
loss is that you also lose your incentive to try new things. It is
safer to stay where you are—to remain in your comfort zone.

To begin to live fully again, you need to step out of your
comfort zone. Start small. Tomorrow, get out of your rut by:

- wearing something bright

- dining at a restaurant you've seen but never tried

- taking a walk or a drive to somewhere you have never
  been before

Life Is Short

Carpe diem (Seize the day)

–Horace, Roman poet

On December 8, 2009, there was an article in *USA Today* which caught my eye.

A worker was killed when a slab of granite fell on him inside a construction supply store. Police said the man, aged forty-seven, was working in the store when the granite fell on his head. The victim's name was withheld pending notification of his family.

We never know when, or how, death will come. We don't know when we wake up in the morning if we will still be around that evening. While this not-knowing may be unsettling, it can also be enlivening. It teaches us that, no matter how long we have on this earth, life is finite and we need to live fully each day.

Losing someone you love awakens you to the fact that you too have limited time on earth. What are you going to do with the time you have left? Are you going to continually mourn your loss or get on with your life?

Life Is a Gift

Reflect upon your present blessings, of which every man has many—not on your past misfortunes, of which all men have some.

—Charles Dickens, English novelist

Look around. What do you have right now?

Sure, you have lost something you love, but you haven't lost everything. If nothing else, if you are still breathing, you have the gift of life.

Perhaps it is time to open that gift and enjoy it.

Help Yourself by Helping Others

*When a man is singing and cannot lift his voice, and
another comes and sings with him, another who
can lift his voice, the first will be able to lift his voice
too. That is the secret of the bond between spirits.*

—Hasidic saying

Author Leo Buscaglia was once asked to judge a contest to
discover the most caring child. The winner was a four-year-
old whose next-door neighbor was an elderly gentleman who
had recently lost his wife. Upon seeing the man cry, the little
boy climbed onto the old gentleman's lap and sat there silently.
When his mother asked what he had said to the neighbor, the
little boy replied, "Nothing, I just helped him cry."

Perhaps the biggest comfort you can give another human
being who is experiencing a loss is to simply be with them. If
laughter comes up when you are with them, laugh. If tears arise
when you are with them, cry.

Spending time with someone who has been through a similar
situation to yours can show you that you too can be a survivor.
As you begin to emerge from your loss, it may be time to help
others with theirs.

God Helps Those Who Help Themselves

Remember, if you ever need a helping hand, you'll find one at the end of your arm…As you grow older you will discover that you have two hands. One for helping yourself, the other for helping others.

–Audrey Hepburn, British actress

Reaching out and helping others is a wonderful way to put your loss in the background. It helps lift you up while doing the same for other people. But you also need to help yourself and make time to nurture and nourish the most important person in your life right now…you.

Get a massage.

Soak in the tub.

Go see an uplifting movie.

Send yourself a greeting card.

Take an afternoon nap.

Allow Others to Do Something for You

None of us has gotten where we are solely by pulling ourselves up from our own bootstraps. We got here because somebody bent down and helped us.

–Thurgood Marshall, US Supreme Court justice

Sometimes we think that it is better to give than receive. While that may be true sometimes, now, in your time of need, it is your turn to receive.

Others may want to do things for you. Allow them to do it.

You may feel that you don't deserve it. You do.

You may feel that you can do it yourself. You can, but let other people help anyway.

Allow other people to:

- cook you a meal
- drive you to an appointment
- take you to an event
- spend time with you
- comfort you

Be Thankful

*He is a man of sense who does not grieve for
what he has not, but rejoices in what he has.*

—Epictetus, Greek philosopher

One of my spiritual teachers would often remind me that, "To want what you don't have is to waste what you do have."

When you are going through a loss, it may feel like everything is lost. It is not. You still have a lot in your life to be thankful for.

Instead of focusing on what you don't have anymore, be grateful for what you do have. Tomorrow morning, before you get out of bed, think of at least one thing that you are thankful for. And then, when you get out of bed, start writing down all the wonderful things in your life. You can be thankful for:

- a penny you found on the street
- the cookies a neighbor brought you
- the friends you have
- a rainbow
- a compliment

- flowers in the park

- a cup of tea

Simple Pleasures

*I have never been a millionaire, but I have
enjoyed a great meal, a crackling fire, a glorious
sunset, a walk with a friend, a hug from a child,
a cup of soup, a kiss behind the ear. There are
plenty of life's tiny delights for all of us.*

—Jack Anthony (attributed)

One action you can take to put your loss in the background for a while is to focus on the little things you like—the little things that bring you joy.

What are the simple little things that bring you pleasure?

- A double latte?

- A certain TV show?

- A visit to your garden?

- Listening to your favorite music?

- The sound of birds chirping?

Half Full or Half Empty?

Some people are always grumbling because roses have thorns. I am thankful that thorns have roses.

—Alphonse Karr, French journalist

You may or may not believe in the power of positive thinking. But even if you don't, what harm would it do to try?

Positive thinking is not about lying to yourself; it is about recognizing what is good about a situation in spite of what you don't like about it.

Tomorrow, catch yourself every time you have a negative thought. Then see if you can find a positive one to replace it.

Shine Your Light

You cannot cause a shadow to disappear by trying to fight it, stomp on it, by railing against it, or any other form of emotional or physical resistance. In order to cause a shadow to disappear, you must shine light on it.

–Shakti Gawain, American teacher/author

The loss you have experienced may have dimmed your enthusiasm for life. But your light hasn't gone out. It just isn't as bright now as it used to be.

Find something to nurture that light.

Find something you love to do.

Find something you can do to help a hurting world.

And you will burn bright again. Perhaps even brighter than before.

A Chance to Rise Higher

Live your life each day as you would climb a mountain. An occasional glance toward the summit keeps the goal in mind, but many beautiful scenes are to be observed from each new vantage point. Climb slowly, steadily, enjoying each passing moment; and the view from the summit will serve as a fitting climax for the journey.

–Harold B. Melchart (attributed)

You may feel down in the dumps. You may feel that you will never rise up from that place. Yet, every day is a chance to move upward.

What can you do today to take one more step on the healing ladder, to take one more step toward living fully again?

Moving On

> *When your car tank is empty, you don't sit and*
> *get depressed and think it's permanent. You*
> *go fill it up. It's the same with life—when you're*
> *running on empty, go fill up your tank with a better*
> *thought, emotion or action and get on with life.*

—Esther Hicks, American author/speaker

Loss often makes you feel like you are stuck. It is paralyzing.
You feel a heaviness weighing you down. You have trouble
moving. You feel you can't possibly go on.

But you can.

If you are reading this book, you are probably ready to move
on. Your loss may feel overwhelming, but now that you have
come this far, you can go further.

Your loss may have thrown you off track for a while, but the
tracks are still there. All you need to do is get back on them.

Yesterday

Don't let yesterday use up too much of today.

–Will Rogers, American humorist

I once heard it said that you can vote on yesterday, but you can't veto it.

What has happened has happened. You can't change that. It is already done.

But you can decide how you will mark your ballot and choose how you will handle things from now on.

Today

Nobody can go back and start a new beginning,
but anyone can start today and make a new ending.

–Maria Robinson (attributed)

Today is really all we have.

Yesterday is a memory. Tomorrow is a fantasy.

No matter how you are feeling today, celebrate it. Today will be gone tomorrow and too late to enjoy.

Live your life today before it becomes yesterday.

Tomorrow

*Courage does not always roar. Sometimes,
it is the quiet voice at the end of the day
saying, "I will try again tomorrow."*

–Mary Anne Radanbacher, American artist/writer

Although your loss may feel overwhelming today, tomorrow may be different.

There are a number of sayings about the hope that tomorrow can bring, such as:

"The sun will come out tomorrow."

"Tomorrow is another day."

"After the rain comes a rainbow."

Such sayings may seem overused and predictable, but still, they are that way because they have a ring of truth about them. No matter how cloudy today might seem to you, the sun will indeed come out tomorrow—or at least the day after, or the one after that. It never stays cloudy forever.

The wonderful thing about life is that each day presents us with a new opportunity to leave yesterday behind.

Time Heals

Time heals all wounds, unless you pick at them.

–Shawn Alexander, American athlete

Another often-heard phrase related to loss is that "time heals everything."

I am not sure that is totally true. Time helps us heal, but perhaps not everything. And perhaps it is not time that is the healer but what we do with that time.

What are you going to do today to help you heal?

Look Around

*Every day we wake up, we are offered the world's
greatest buffet. It spreads as far as the eye can
see with vats of pleasure and joy, laughter and
smiles, happiness and contentment. It is available
to all. It is bought and paid for. Yet we take
only a tiny salad plate to this fabulous spread
and serve ourselves a few mere morsels.*

–Susan Sparks, American spiritual teacher

Several years ago, as an experiment, the world-renowned
violinist Joshua Bell played at the entrance to one of the world's
busiest subway stations. What the researchers discovered was
the sad fact that few people took the opportunity to stop and
hear this incredible free concert. Most rushed by, ignoring
a rare, once-in-a-lifetime opportunity to hear Bell play on a
violin worth $3.5 million.

There is such an abundance of joyful things in this world, yet
most of us don't stop and hear the music—or smell the roses—
even when it is right in front of us.

Stop for a few moments today and look around you.

What have you missed seeing in your environment that can
bring you more joy and help you to live more fully?

Bitter-Sweetness of Life

> *A man traveling across a field encountered a tiger.*
> *He fled, the tiger after him. Coming to a precipice,*
> *he caught hold of the root of a wild vine and swung*
> *himself down over the edge. The tiger sniffed at him*
> *from above. Trembling, the man looked down to where,*
> *far below, another tiger was waiting to eat him. Only*
> *the vine sustained him. Meanwhile, two mice started to*
> *gnaw away the vine. The man saw a luscious strawberry*
> *near him. Grasping the vine with one hand, he plucked*
> *the strawberry with the other. How sweet it tasted!*

—The Buddha

In the midst of loss, life may seem unsettling and bitter. That, at times, may be true. But life, at times, is also sweet. The bittersweet quality of life is ever present.

Like Buddha's parable above, we can have danger and the presence of death nearby, yet still find sweetness in life.

Can you reach out today to pluck a strawberry and find some sweetness among the sadness?

Life Goes On

*I have found that life persists in the midst of
destruction and, therefore, there must be
a higher law than that of destruction.*

–Mahatma Gandhi, Indian spiritual leader

In the play *The Skin of Our Teeth*, Thornton Wilder writes about the Antrobus family, who suffer incredible devastation as they combat all the horrors that befell man throughout the ages. They battle dinosaurs, they deal with Ice Age flooding, and they confront famine and plagues. In each case, they survive by "the skin of their teeth."

In spite of all the hardships the family endures, one of the characters strongly advises us "not to inquire why or whither, but just enjoy your ice cream while it's on your plate."

Can you take that advice to heart today and enjoy your ice cream before it melts?

Additional Thoughts on Living

*It's only when we truly know and understand
that we have a limited time on earth—and that
we have no way of knowing when our time is
up—that we will begin to live each day to the
fullest, as if it was the only one we had.*

—Elisabeth Kübler-Ross, Swiss-born psychiatrist

*When someone we love dies, we get so busy
mourning what died that we ignore what didn't.*

—Ram Dass, spiritual teacher

*I like living. I have sometimes been wildly,
despairingly, acutely miserable, racked with
sorrow, but through it all I still know quite
certainly that just to be alive is a grand thing.*

—Agatha Christie, British writer

Step Five

Laughing

> *Tragedy and comedy are but two aspects of what is real, and whether we see the tragic or the humorous is a matter of perspective.*
>
> **–Arnold Beisser, polio-disabled American author**

It may seem ludicrous putting laughter and loss in the same sentence. How can you possibly laugh after losing a loved one? Yet research by Dacher Keltner and George A. Bonanno shows that the more widows and widowers laughed and smiled during the early months after their spouse's death, the better their mental health was over the first two years of bereavement.

Laughter is a great coping mechanism. Finding the humor in anything and laughing about it gives you a break from the pain of loss. It allows for a breath of fresh air at a time when everything seems dark and heavy.

Many of the world's top comedians intuitively knew this when they experienced a major loss in their life. They turned to humor to cope and eventually perfected their craft and made comedy their career.

Your goal is probably not to become a stand-up comic, but you can take a lesson from these renowned comedians and use humor and laughter to help you to cope with your loss.

Laughter and humor are among God's gifts to overcome your trials and tribulations.

Laughter and Tears

*And the self-same well from which your laughter
rises was oftentimes filled with your tears.*

–Kahlil Gibran, Lebanese/American poet

It is okay to cry. Tears wash away harmful toxins in your body that build up when you are stressed and grieving. They help cleanse and wash away your sorrow.

But tears can also stop you from embracing and enjoying life. At some point, you need to curtail your crying in order to get on with your life.

When you stop crying, it doesn't mean that you loved the person you lost any less, or that you have forgotten them. It only means that you are ready to put your loss in the background for a while and let life unfold again.

And that involves learning to live and, yes, even laugh again.

Appropriate, Timely, and Tasteful

> *If humor is something like a sword, maybe it has to be strapped on, but nobody should go around without it in any period of time.... Since one of its chief constituents is taste, it should be used sparingly sometimes and left in its sheath at other times, but it should always be handy.*

—James Thurber, American author

A long time ago, a friend of mine was having a difficult time dealing with the breakup of a long-term relationship. He was explaining what had happened between him and his partner. I tried cheering him up and offered a lighthearted remark or two, which, I learned later, offended him. He didn't think I took his "serious situation" seriously enough.

When you feel like crying, you often don't feel like laughing. In fact, when you are in those down times, anything funny may seem offensive.

While laughter can be beneficial during and after a loss, you may not be ready for it. Don't force it. Just know that even though your lighter side is in hiding right now, it is still there and may appear when you least expect it.

How Can You Laugh at a Time like This?

I think laughter may be a form of courage.
As humans we sometimes stand tall and look
into the sun and laugh, and I think we are
never more brave than when we do that.

–Linda Ellerbee, American journalist

Many people feel guilty when they laugh during a loss. They ask, "How can you laugh at a time like this?" Since laughter can be as healing as tears, the question, perhaps, should really be, "How can you *not* laugh at a time like this?"

If something funny happens, laugh. If something funny doesn't happen, don't laugh. Just don't ignore the laughter when something strikes your funny bone.

Sometimes, people feel guilty for laughing when someone has died, or when they are dealing with a life-challenging situation. As long as you are not laughing at the deceased, the grieving, or the ill person, laughter can be as healing as tears.

Allow for both the tears and the laughter.

Don't Compare

*Laughter has always brought me out of
unhappy situations. Even in your darkest
moment, you usually can find something to
laugh about if you try hard enough.*

—Red Skelton, American comedian

Every person's funny bone is in a different place. I love Steve
Martin for his laidback, often illogical, kind of comedy. Other
people might like the put-down humor of Don Rickles, or
the absurd humor of stand-up comedian Steve Wright, or the
family-friendly humor of Jerry Seinfeld.

Who, or what, makes you laugh? Get more of those people, or
things, in your life.

Humor Buddies

*Let us be grateful to people who make us
happy; they are the charming gardeners
who make our souls blossom.*

–Marcel Proust, French novelist

I laugh a lot with some people. I hardly laugh at all with others.

Find those people—friends, acquaintances, cartoonists, comedians, or entertainers—who bring a smile to your face

If they are friends, colleagues, or acquaintances, call them now.

If they are professional comedians or comic actors, watch one of their movies or TV shows.

If they are cartoonists, keep their cartoons where you can see them often.

Give It Time

Comedy is tragedy plus time.

–Carol Burnett, American comedian

As noted earlier, it has been said that time heals everything.

That doesn't mean that you will ever forget your loved one. What it means is that, in time, your loss will not seem as enormous as it does now.

What it also means is that at some point, it will be possible to laugh again.

Open to Laughter

Lightness of touch and living in the moment are intertwined. One cannot dance well unless one is completely in time with the music, not leaning back to the last step or pressing forward to the next one, but poised directly on the present step as it comes.

–Anne Morrow Lindbergh, American aviator/author

There is always something to laugh about. The problem is that when we are stressed out, or in the grieving process, we may not see it. But it is still there. Something funny might be right next to us but, like a horse with blinders, we don't see or hear it because we are only focusing on our loss.

Take off those blinders. Be open to laughter. And don't squelch it when it comes because, as comedian Fred Allen reminds us, "It is bad to suppress laughter. It goes back down and spreads to your hips."

Laughter and Loss

> *Life does not cease to be funny when people die any more than it ceases to be serious when people laugh.*

—George Bernard Shaw, Irish dramatist

Serious illness, death, dying, and tragedies are no laughing matter. Things happen that aren't funny. Still, funny things happen.

If you think they don't, consider:

- the hospital gown ("Now I know why they call it ICU")
- an open casket where someone says, "She never looked so good."
- a tombstone that reads, "See, I told you I was sick."

To Laugh Again

*Be of good cheer. Do not think of today's failures,
but of the success that may come tomorrow.
You have set yourselves a difficult task, but
you will succeed if you persevere; and you
will find a joy in overcoming obstacles.*

—Helen Keller, American blind/deaf author

Because of the intense loss you are experiencing, you may feel
that you have also lost your sense of humor. You haven't lost it.
It is just misplaced. You can, and will, find it again.

Keep looking.

Today, tell yourself that you will find one little thing of hope,
one little thing that amuses you, one little thing to smile or
laugh about.

If you can do that, you have taken a big step in your
healing process.

Let It Begin With You

*Beginning with the early dawn each day, I will radiate
joy to everyone I meet. I will be mental sunshine for
all who cross my path. I will burn candles of smiles
in the bosoms of the joyless. Before the unfading
light of my cheer, darkness will take flight.*

—Paramahansa Yogananda, Indian mediation teacher

If you are to find any joy in your life after your loss, it must
begin with you. Others can guide you and show you the
way, but they cannot do it for you. You need to find that joy
inside yourself.

Perhaps you can begin with a smile.

Start With a Smile

Sometimes your joy is the source of your smile, but sometimes your smile can be the source of your joy.

–Thich Nhat Hanh, Buddhist monk

After a loss, it may take time to regain your laughter. That is understandable. It may even be difficult to smile. But that is a good place to start, since research has shown that smiling produces effects conducive to healing. It has been theorized that smiling creates cooler blood, resulting in sensations of calm and happiness. Frowning, on the other hand, creates warmer blood, resulting in feelings of sadness and anger.

So, smile when you wake up because the sun is shining.

Smile when you wake up because it is raining. Smile because you wake up.

Healing Humor

Always laugh when you can. It is cheap medicine.

—Lord Byron, English poet

Healing doesn't mean that you are cured. It means that you are moving toward, getting better. The Old English definition of healing means to restore to sound health. And that is what a little laughter can do.

The crying times may still come, but a little laughter from time to time can help you get some distance from your loss and help heal your wounds.

Tension Release

*Laughter lets me relax. It's the equivalent
of taking a deep breath, letting it out
and saying, "This too will pass."*

—Odette Pollar, American author

When someone is dying, feelings are often raw, conversations stilted, and emotions run high. One of the important benefits of finding something funny, even in a crisis, is that laughter eases tensions and brings people together.

For example, one hospice nurse arrived at a family's home just after they put the patient on a bedside commode. While the nurse and the family were in the room, the patient had a bowel movement that was accompanied by a lot of loud noises. At first, everyone pretended that they heard nothing. Then, a young grandchild, overwhelmed by the smell, yelled out, "Geeesh, Grandma!" and quickly ran out of the room. Everyone erupted in laughter. The incident broke the tension and created a bonding among the family. From then on, the nurse observed, the family shared easily.

Humor and Survival

He who laughs, lasts.

–Mary Pettibone Poole, author (attributed)

We don't often think of humor and laughter as a survival mechanism. We forget that when we "laugh it off," we are actually doing just that.

If you can laugh, even just a little, it shows you that there is light at the end of the tunnel.

A little bit of laughter shows you that you can go on…

That you will survive.

The Power of Humor

*A sense of humor...is needed armor. Joy in one's
heart and some laughter on one's lips is a sign that the
person down deep has a pretty good grasp on life.*

—Hugh Sidey, American journalist

When you can find something to laugh about during your
grieving process, you have taken a step toward freeing yourself
from that loss.

Laughter frees us. When we laugh, we are no longer engulfed
in our sorrow. We have broken free and affirmed that we
can rise above our circumstance. The smallest amount of
laughter can show you that you are not permanently stuck in a
downward spiral. You can, even if only momentarily, start that
climb up again.

No one has the power to stop death. But we all have the power
to laugh in the face of it and not let death take away our joy
of living.

As one author noted, "With laughter, death is less of a
grave matter."

The Power to Rise Above

*Humor is an affirmation of dignity, a declaration
of man's superiority to all that befalls him.*

—Romain Gary, French writer

Viktor Frankl used humor to give him hope during his
incarceration in a German concentration camp.

Captain Gerald Coffee used humor to deal with his seven-year
confinement as a prisoner of war in North Vietnam.

Kathy Buckley, Alex Valdez, and Brett Leake are, respectively,
deaf, blind, and a person with muscular dystrophy. All of them
rise above what life has handed them by using humor in their
stand-up comedy acts.

If they can find something to laugh about in their challenging
situations, you can too.

Softening the Blow

For me, if you are able to laugh,
you are the owner of the world.

—Roberto Benigni, Italian actor

You have been hit with a loss. Humor and laughter will never change that. But they can soften the blow.

A good laugh can:

- divert your thinking away from your troubles

- balance your sadness

- connect you to other people

- help you calm down

- make you feel that life is worth living

Dealing with a major loss is draining. You may feel like you are running on empty. Finding something to laugh about, even for just a few seconds, can help to fill you up again.

Laughter is the juice of life. Squeeze all the energy you can out of it.

Finding Happiness Again

The way to happiness: keep your heart free from hate, your mind from worry. Live simply, expect little, give much. Fill your life with love. Scatter sunshine. Forget self, think of others. Do as you would be done by. Try this for a week and you will be surprised.

–Norman Vincent Peale, minister/author

After your loss, it may seem that you will never be happy again. It may seem that way right now, but that is only now.

Looking back in ten days, ten weeks, ten months, or ten years, you will probably feel differently about your loss than you do today.

Can you even imagine what your life will be like in those future days, weeks, months, or years? It may be difficult for you to see yourself as being happy during that time. But happiness is available. Wait. You'll see.

Uplifting Words

Loving words cost but little
journeying up the hill of life;
But they make the weak and weary
Stronger, braver, for the strife.
Do you count them only trifles
What to earth are sun and rain?
Never was a kind word wasted;
Never was one said in vain.

—Anonymous

Words are powerful. They can lift you up. They can bring you down. What you are reading now has the power to heal and change your thinking. Similarly, the words you constantly say to yourself are equally as powerful to heal.

Watch what you say today and notice if your words are helping you overcome your loss or bringing you further down into it.

Look for words that lift your spirit, that make your heart sing, and fill you with joy. Words such as:

- Amusing
- Cheery
- Delightful

- Enjoyable
- Happy
- Hopeful
- Jolly
- Joyful
- Laughing
- Merry
- Pleasing
- Pleasurable
- Smiling
- **Wonderful**

Positive Self-Talk

Watch your thoughts, for they become words.
Watch your words, for they become actions.
Watch your actions, for they become habits.
Watch your habits, for they become character.
Watch your character, for it becomes your destiny.

–Anonymous

What you tell yourself about your loss is a good indicator of how you will recover from it. Are you telling yourself, "I will pull through this somehow," or are you saying, "I will never get over this"?

What you say to yourself is often self-prophesizing. Tell yourself that you are on the road to healing and every day you will get closer to that goal. Or, continually tell yourself that you will never stop grieving and you will carry around your suffering forever.

In each case, what are you telling yourself about your loss?

All That Is Left

*Humor prevents one from becoming a tragic figure
even though he/she is involved in tragic events.*

–E. T. "Cy" Eberhart, American hospital chaplain

When I was a volunteer with hospice, I would see patients who could not do any of the things that had once come so easily to them. They had trouble eating, bathing, and dressing themselves. Everything had been taken from them. Sometimes all they had left was their sense of humor.

The same is often true when one has experienced a loss. In her book, *Laugh Your Way to Grace*, author Susan Sparks writes about speaking to a woman who lost her husband on 9/11. In describing him in detail for a missing persons report, the woman said, "Oh, I forgot to tell you, he left the house with the worst tie on! It was like this horrible green color with flamingos and palm trees."

Realizing what she just said, the woman started to laugh. After a moment of silence, the woman told Sparks, "You must think me crazy laughing like this." After the pause, the woman whispered, "But laughter is all my family and I have left."

If that is all you feel you have left, then laugh—and make it loud and long.

Anesthesia for the Heart

*Cartoons and humor are not for the good times.
They're for all the bad frustrations, annoyances,
and things bordering on the horrible that happen
to us. And they're even for the horrible things
[that] happen to other people—it's a certain little
anesthesia of the heart which is necessary.*

—Bob Mankoff, cartoon editor of the New Yorker

Humor is all around us. Every day there are opportunities to laugh about something.

Take some time today and find one thing—just one thing—that amuses you and makes you laugh, even for a short while. It will provide some anesthesia for your heart.

If all you can do is smile loudly, that's okay too.

God-Given Laughter

Laughter is the God in us.

—C. McNair Wilson, American author

It has been said that God never gives you more than you can handle. It is also true that God has given you a tool to help you handle what is given to you. That tool is your sense of humor and laughter.

And if you don't think God has a playful sense of humor, consider:

- the platypus
- the giraffe
- the hippopotamus

Just Laugh

Even if there is nothing to laugh about, laugh on credit.

—Anonymous

Participants in laughter clubs, which started in India, get together on a regular basis to laugh. There are no jokes told, no funny stories shared—only people laughing. They don't have a reason to laugh. They just do it.

You can do it too.

Humor and Hope

*I have seen what a laugh can do. It can
transform almost unbearable tears into
something bearable, even hopeful.*

—Bob Hope, American comedian

Hope is the greatest treasure you have.

When all else fails, hope is something to hang onto.

Don't give up.

And there is a strong connection between humor, hope, and laughter. When you can find something to laugh about, you are saying that there is hope for the future.

Laughter implies that you can go on.

Laughter implies that you will go on.

If you can find something to laugh about, even for just a few seconds, it is a sign that you can survive your situation.

If you can laugh for a moment,

you can laugh for a moment more,

and a moment after that one too.

Additional Thoughts on Laughing

You can just as easily laugh and play while you grow as become serious and overwhelmed.

—Gary Zukav, American author

To become conscious of what is horrifying and to laugh at it is to become master of that which is horrifying.

—Eugene Ionesco, Romanian/French playwright

A sense of humor can help you overlook the unattractive, tolerate the unpleasant, cope with the unexpected, and smile through the unbearable.

—Moshe Waldoks, American spiritual teacher

Time for Some Laughs?

I'm not a fan of jokes. I'd rather find humor in everyday situations, but that is sometimes hard to do, especially when you are dealing with a loss. Jokes are also very subjective; you may not find something funny that I think is hysterical, and vice versa.

That said, if you're having trouble finding something to laugh about, here, to help you get started, are some of my favorite jokes in the death and dying arena. Please feel free to skip this section if you are not ready for or open to jokes at this time. I understand.

***

A very old man lay dying in his bed. Suddenly he smelled the aroma of his favorite chocolate chip cookie. He gathered his strength and lifted himself from the bed. He slowly made his way out of the bedroom and forced himself down the stairs.

With labored breath, he looked into the kitchen. He thought he was already in heaven. There, spread out on the kitchen table were literally hundreds of his favorite cookie.

Was this heaven? Or was it one final act of love from his devoted wife, seeing to it that he left this world a happy man?

Mustering all his strength, he moved toward the table. His shaking hand made its way to a cookie, when he was suddenly smacked with a spatula by his wife.

"Stay away from those," she said. "They're for the funeral!"

***

Two hunters are out in the woods when one of them collapses. He doesn't seem to be breathing and his eyes are glazed. The other guy whips out his phone and calls the emergency services. He gasps, "My friend is dead! What can I do?"

The operator says, "Calm down. I can help. First, let's make sure he's dead."

There is a silence; then a gunshot is heard. Back on the phone, the guy says, "Okay, now what?"

***

Two cannibals are eating a clown, when one cannibal looks up and asks the other one, "Does he taste funny to you?"

***

A woman's husband, Robert, had been slipping in and out of a coma for several months. Still, she had stayed by his bedside every single day.

One day, when he came to, he motioned for her to come nearer.

As she sat by him, he whispered, eyes full of tears, "You know what? You have been with me all through the bad times. When I got fired, you were there to support me. When my business failed, you were there. When I got shot, you were by my side. When we lost the house, you stayed right here. When my health started failing, you were still by my side. You know what, Gloria?"

"What, Robert?" she asked, smiling as her heart began to fill with love.

"I'm beginning to think you're bad luck."

***

A wife decided to leave for a vacation, leaving her husband in supervision of her mother and her cat. After a few days, she called her husband and asked, "How is everything going?" He responded with, "The cat is dead."

She cried out and said, "Why couldn't you've broken the news slowly? You could have said the cat is playing on the roof on the first day, and the next say it broke its leg, then the next that the poor thing's dead! Anyways, how's my mom?"

"She's playing on the roof."

***

When I die, I want to go peacefully like my grandfather did, in his sleep—not screaming, like the passengers in his car.

Closing Diary

Sunday, April 13

It is the day of Bernice's unveiling. (In the Jewish tradition, an unveiling is a graveside ceremony within a year of a person's death. It dedicates the grave marker and gives those in mourning a chance to once more honor the deceased.)

It is a somewhat chilly and blustery day in New Jersey. But we are thankful that the forecasted heavy rain did not materialize. We gather around Bernice's low footstone that is covered by a cloth held down with a small stone at each corner.

The service starts with the traditional blessings by the rabbi. Then, friends and family add their eulogies. Some go on much too long. A number of those gathered seem anxious for the service to conclude. Several times, a strong wind comes up and nearly blows the cloth away.

When this happens, those gathered around look at each other with a slight grin. All probably thinking a similar thought— Bernice's spirit is telling us that it is time to end the service. We could almost hear her saying, "Stop mourning me." Like the wind blowing the cloth away, it is time to move on. It is time to get on with life.

Moving On

I trust you have received some comfort and encouragement from reading this book. I have found that one of the most powerful ways of getting the most value out of something is to write down my thoughts about what I've experienced. I therefore encourage you to enhance what you have read by responding to the following questions. This small bit of journaling will give you a chance and a place to write down your responses. Hopefully, it will deepen your understanding of your loss and its place in your life.

P.S. Please note that this is not a test. You will not be graded. And, there are no right or wrong answers.

What are you grateful for in your life right now?

. . . .

_____

_____

_____

_____

_____

_____

_____

_____

_____

_____

_____

_____

_____

_____

_____

_____

_____

_____

_____

_____

_____

_____

_____

_____

_____

_____

_____

_____

_____

What has helped you deal with previous losses?

· ·

_____

_____

_____

_____

_____

_____

_____

_____

_____

_____

_____

_____

_____

_____

_____

_____

_____

_____

_____

_____

_____

_____

_____

_____

_____

_____

_____

How do you see your life in five, ten, and fifteen years?

· ·

_____

_____

_____

_____

_____

_____

_____

_____

_____

_____

_____

_____

_____

_____

_____

_____

_____

_____

_____

_____

_____

_____

_____

_____

_____

_____

_____

_____

_____

_____

What have you learned from dealing with loss?

· · · · · · · · · · · · · · · · · ·

_____

_____

_____

_____

_____

_____

_____

_____

_____

_____

_____

_____

_____

_____

_____

_____

How will you keep the memory of the person you lost alive?

· ·

_____

_____

_____

_____

_____

_____

_____

_____

_____

_____

_____

_____

_____

_____

_____

_____

_____

_____

_____

_____

_____

_____

_____

_____

_____

_____

_____

_____

What can you forgive yourself or others for that would help you move on?

· ·

_____

_____

_____

_____

_____

_____

_____

_____

_____

_____

_____

_____

_____

_____

_____

_____

_____

_____

_____

_____

_____

_____

_____

_____

_____

_____

_____

_____

How are you going to flourish and take better care of yourself?

· ·

_____

_____

_____

_____

_____

_____

_____

_____

_____

_____

_____

_____

_____

_____

_____

_____

_____

_____

_____

_____

_____

_____

_____

_____

_____

_____

_____

_____

In what ways can you celebrate the life of the person you lost?

· ·

_____

_____

_____

_____

_____

_____

_____

_____

_____

_____

_____

_____

_____

_____

_____

_____

_____

_____

_____

_____

_____

_____

_____

_____

_____

_____

_____

What are some of the fond or funny memories you have of the deceased?

. . . .

_____

_____

_____

_____

_____

_____

_____

_____

_____

_____

_____

_____

_____

_____

_____

_____

_____

_____

_____

_____

_____

_____

_____

_____

_____

_____

_____

How are you going to get more joy and laughter in your life?

· ·

_____

_____

_____

_____

_____

_____

_____

_____

_____

_____

_____

_____

_____

_____

Suggested Reading

There are lots of books on dealing with both loss and the meaning of life. Some of my favorites are:

Bach, Richard. *Illusions*. New York: Dell Publishing, 1979.

Broyard, Anatole. *Intoxicated by My Illness*. New York: Fawcett Columbine, 1992.

Canfield, a k, et al. *Chicken Soup for the Grieving Soul*. Deerfield Beach, FL: Health Communications, 1993.

Canfield, a k, et al. *Chicken Soup for the Surviving Soul*. Deerfield Beach, FL: Health Communications, 1996.

Carlton, Richard. *Don't Sweat the Small Stuff...and it's all small stuff*. New York: Hyperion, 1997.

Colgrove, Melba, et. al. *How to Survive the Loss of a Love*. New York: Leo Press, 1976.

Grollman, Earl. *When Your Loved One is Dying*. Boston: Beacon Press, 1980.

Klein, Allen. *The Healing Power of Humor*. Los Angeles: J. P. Tarcher, 1989.

Klein, Allen. *The Courage to Laugh*. Los Angeles: New York: J.P. Tarcher/Putnam, 1998.

Kushner, Harold S. *When Bad Things Happen to Good People*. New York: Schocken Books, 1981.

Levine, Stephen. *Who Dies*? Garden City, NY: Anchor Press/Doubleday, 1982.

Prather, Hugh. *Notes to Myself*. Moab, UT: Real People Press, 1970.

Tatelbaum, Judy. *The Courage to Grieve*. New York: Lippincott & Crowell, 1980.

Welshons, John. *Awakening from Grief*. Little Falls, NJ: Open Heart Publications, 2000.

Wilder, Thornton. *Our Town: A Play in Three Acts*. New York: Coward-McCann, in cooperation with S. French, 1965.

About the Author

Allen Klein is a former director of The Life-Death Transitions Institute in San Francisco. Currently he is an award-winning professional speaker and best-selling author. Klein is a recipient of a Lifetime Achievement Award from the Association for Applied and Therapeutic Humor, a Certified Speaking Professional designation from the National Speakers Association, a Communication and Leadership Award from Toastmasters International, and an inductee in the Hunter College, New York City, Hall of Fame.

Klein is also the author of twenty-six books including *The Healing Power of Humor, The Courage to Laugh, Change Your Life!: A Little Book of Big Ideas, Secrets Kids Know*, and *You Can't Ruin My Day*. He is also a TEDx presenter.

For more information about Klein's books or presentations, go to www.allenklein.com or contact him at: allen@allenklein.com.